D1565679

THE WAKE

An Irish Ghost Story

NP CUNNIFFE

SB
SCARYBOOKS

"Unexpressed emotions will never die. They are buried alive and will come forth later in uglier ways."

Sigmund Freud

CONTENTS

I

He waited in the car as he watched the last of the mourners disappear into the shadows of the house. The engine was still running, keeping him warm. Snowflakes settled on the windscreen, before melting slowly and sliding down the glass, leaving soft white tears in their wake.

He hated the snow. It made him anxious, made his heart race and his hands tremble. He gripped the steering wheel tight, watched the scars on his knuckles burn red, and told himself the snow would pass. It always did.

Not this time.

He turned on the radio for the seven o'clock local obituaries. Although, if he didn't go in soon, he may not be allowed inside at all. Still, he decided he'd wait until he heard her name announced. He'd only received the solicitor's letter days before he was due to fly, inviting him to a reading of the will.

He still couldn't quite believe it. But he'd read her name correctly, along with a letter from his parents saying they'd also be attending the wake.

Callahan.

He could see her name now on the windscreen, the scrawling ink jet black against the snow. He'd almost forgotten about her.

Almost.

"Paddy Finan," the newsreader announced. The name woke him from his thoughts. "Headford, Co. Galway. Sunday, 22nd December, peacefully at his home in his eighty-sixth year."

He didn't know any Paddy Finan. Still, he listened attentively, as he'd always done when he heard the obituaries on the radio, even if it was a repeat. He had never been to any Irish household that didn't fall silent when obituaries sounded from a nearby radio. It was a tradition he could never shake, no matter where he was in the world. Whenever he heard the death notices on a local radio, he would pause whatever he was doing and bow his head. It was a sign of respect for the dead, and it wasn't much to be asked.

"But why can't we talk?" he'd once asked his mother as a very young child. A toddler, perhaps, as he got ready for play-school.

"Because they could be listening," she scowled, fastening his little shoes with the velcro straps. "And they won't be too happy if you keep talking!"

"Teresa Callahan," the radio announced. His ears pricked up. "Ballycolgan, Co. Galway. Monday 23rd December, peacefully at home, aged sixty-three. Reposing at her home Thursday from four o'clock until half past six. Funeral Mass will take place Friday morning in St. Patrick's Church at eleven o'clock. Burial afterwards in the adjoining cemetery."

He wondered if she had any family. Was that the reason he was being called to her will reading? He'd never seen any visitors inside her house, except her students. Would they be inside now? The thought made him feel sick. Could he avoid them, somehow?

He waited until the notices had finished before looking over the wheel. Only one window was lit – the front room, or parlour, as she liked to call it. That's where she lay. Dead. Waiting. He hadn't stepped inside that house in years. Before university and the Masters. Before the bad days got worse.

Figures moved behind the curtains, around her body. They were leaving from the back of the house, shuffling silently through the snow to their cars. Some had even arrived on tractors. The countryside never changed. There was always farming to be done, even on the blackest of days.

He kept a close eye on those leaving, waiting for the best opportunity, counting the time between them. Fifteen seconds at most. He couldn't deal with any nosy neighbours now, all wondering what she'd left him in her will. At least, not before he'd seen the body. In and out, unless his parents were inside. They never missed a wake in the parish.

He had attended many wakes as a child, which always involved a lot of hanging around the deceased's house. Strange, really. Why not throw a huge gathering while the individual was still alive? Hours would be spent sitting next to the coffin on his father's knees, cups of tea being passed from hand to hand as the damp, sickly smell emanating from the corpse tickled his nose. Once he got so bored, he slipped from his father's knee and walked over to an old dead lady before lifting her skirt, feeling the clammy skin inside, much to the horror of all the mourners. His mother had dragged him into the hallway after that and told him he "must never touch dead people again."

"Why not?" he'd asked. "They're dead anyway and not going to feel it."

"Because," she'd sighed, both hands clasped around his little shoulders. "Because she could be watching us, from up above. Or her soul could still be trapped inside her, waiting until we've said enough prayers to get her into heaven. So the last thing she'll want are little boys poking at her dead body."

Would his mother be inside now?

He turned off the radio, took a breath, and then pulled on the door.

The snow was soft beneath his feet. He let the door close quietly behind him and then followed the mourners' footprints to the door, both large and small, and kept his head down. He could see his breath before him, captured in the light from the front room. The car had read minus temperatures on the drive from the airport. It was an unusually cold December – most Decembers were now mild in Ireland. But the air was painfully cold, cutting his lips and stabbing his chest from within. He clutched his chest tight, felt his heart beating rapidly inside. His breathing grew quick. Shallow. His doctor had prescribed him anti-anxiety pills for exactly this. How had he forgotten to take them? And on a night like this? All those people. All those faces. Their probing eyes searching him. *Why had he been left something?* they would wonder. Should he go back to the car now? Take a few pills first?

Too late, he thought, his shoe kicking into the doorstep.

He stopped, closing his eyes. Slowly, he inhaled through his nose. His chest stabbed with pain. That was always expected. After eight seconds, he let the air pass from his lips. He would repeat this several times, hoping no one would see. They'd probably think he was mad, or worse, meditating.

A tractor hummed in the distance. He listened to it fade, driving into the deep of the countryside. Finally, he opened his eyes, shook the snow from his shoes and his shoulders, and pressed down on the door handle.

The first thing he noticed was the smell of incense. It smelt like smoke, or ash, and reminded him of priests blessing the altar during the funeral masses many years ago. Fainter came the smell of cigarettes, heavily masked by the incense. The house had always smelled of cigarettes, leaving its foul odour in its guests' clothes for days.

He closed the door behind him, catching his thin reflection in the mirror on the wall. His face looked more gaunt than usual, and paler. Or perhaps it was this mirror he was all too familiar with, magnifying each tiny difference?

Still, he looked closer. His cheekbones cast slanted shadows across his face, replacing the chubby cheeks he once had. His dark brown hair was long and greasy, bulging from underneath his cap, covering his eyes.

He removed his cap and brushed his fringe out of the way, revealing dark-blue circles beneath his eyes. He'd planned to sleep on the plane but knew it wouldn't be possible – he could never sleep on flights, despite taking his pills. Besides, the turbulence of flying into the west of Ireland would keep anyone awake. Inspecting closer, he noticed he was sweating, the beads forming streaks down his white skin, making him look glassy, almost deathly. He pulled a handkerchief from inside his coat and quickly mopped up the sweat. He couldn't show he was sweating. He wouldn't dare show any nerves.

Pocketing the damp handkerchief, he turned towards the stairs and, almost instinctively, stepped over the creaky floorboard. Whispers travelled down the hall. Prayers and condolences, he imagined. His heart suddenly leapt in his chest. What would he say? What was expected of him to say? He wasn't a child anymore, at least in his eyes. He had to act the grown-up now. Express his sorrow. Express his grief. He couldn't play with all the other children now, exploring each nook and cranny in the house, discovering every peculiarity of the deceased. No. He had to actually show that he was sorry. And not just sorry, genuinely sorry too. He'd never done that before; at least as an adult. Why hadn't he thought of this before? He could've practised. He'd had time. Instead, he'd been thinking about seeing his parents all this time, understandably – he only flew home around Christmas. But still, he should have taken a moment to research how an adult must act at a wake...

"Michael?"

It came in a whisper, barely brushing his ear. It was only then he realised he'd been staring at the grandfather clock by the stairs. The handles were stuck at four-thirty.

The time of death.

"We're in here."

He turned around to find a pair of emerald eyes sparkling from the room behind him. It was Molly. She was standing just inside the door of the front room, her arms folded, chestnut-brown hair falling in waves down her crimson jumper. He moved towards her, almost tripping on the flaps of his coat. He attempted a smile to soften his clumsiness, but she didn't return it. In fact, he thought he saw tears in her eyes. The rims underneath were red, accentuated by her jumper. Another student of the deceased.

"Good to see you," she uttered, patting Michael's arm gently. He didn't know what to say, so continued to smile. But was a smile suitable on this occasion? Or would it be too much, too exuberant? He hardened his face as much as he could, before continuing into the room. "Talk to you in a bit, yeah?" she whispered. He looked back and nodded.

Mourners sat all around the room, around the open coffin, their chairs lining the walls. He scanned each sorrowful face, hoping to spot his parents. A child of about five or six was crying from a corner, his mother trying to hush him. An elderly woman in a purple, woolly hat – far too big for her head – threw out her hand to him without looking up. He shivered as he felt his fingers sliding over protruding veins, like lumps and bumps on a once-smooth road.

"Mammy, why are Granddad's hands so veiny?" he remembered asking his mother at his grandparents' cottage one winter, as he sat on his own hands, keeping them warm.

"That's what happens when you sit on your hands," his mother hissed at him, before he jumped off his chair and shook his hands in disgust. Even though he had his doubts about his mother's theory, he had never sat on his hands since. He couldn't get the image of the veins out of his head, protruding like gnarly roots underneath a tree, breaking through the surface. Surely his own hands would never look like that, even if he had continued sitting on them? Still, he wasn't taking any chances.

Someone coughed beside him, waking him from his thoughts. He pulled his hand away before moving on, keeping his eyes firmly away from the centre of the room. Instead, he kept his eyes on his hands, still smooth and blemish-free, nothing like his grandfather's or the old woman's.

Another elderly lady held her hand out to him. She was petite, like the woman next to her, but without the hat. He wondered if they were sisters. She gripped his hands tight, muttering something incoherent under her breath.

"Yes, I'm sorry," he uttered, remembering he must say something to these people, before pulling his hand away as quickly as he could, which required more effort than he expected. He wanted to get through this quickly, and with as little handshaking as possible.

By the time he was at the window, he had remembered some utterances from his childhood – "Sorry for your loss," "Sorry for your trouble," "Condolences to you and your family," that sort of thing – and had exhausted many of these phrases by the time he eventually made his way back to the door.

"Very, very sorry," he finally said.

"You're alright," a white-haired man in a suit and tie muttered, patting him hard on the shoulder without looking up, which he much preferred to another veiny handshake. "It's just good to see you, Michael. Welcome back."

He wasn't sure if he knew this man,

though he supposed everyone must know who he was. It was a small parish, after all. Everyone knew everyone. Or at least, everyone but Michael knew everyone.

"Yeah, you too," Michael said, offering a smile.

He looked up at Molly, who seemed to be waiting for him.

"They're all in the kitchen," she said, pointing behind her as if he'd forgotten. He'd never forget this house. Sometimes, it would appear in his dreams; the long, dark halls sneaking up on him and swallowing him whole, including everything else he was dreaming about. He could never rid himself of this house, no matter how much he tried. He could never forget the smell either, a waft of cigarette smoke finding him in the quietest recesses of the library. Perhaps this time he could say goodbye to the house for good.

"Come on," she said, guiding him from the room, past the stairs. The bannisters, he noticed, were decorated with white flowers, possibly lilies. Perhaps someone thought the stairs looked too gloomy, sitting in the dark corner of the old house, leading all the way up to the...

No, he thought, turning his head towards the kitchen. He wouldn't look up there. Up there remained in the past, with its many rooms and dark corners. Soon to be buried, along with the dead.

He followed Molly down the hall towards the back of the house, hoping to find his parents there. Smoke seeped from the walls the further he walked. The air smelled mustier than he remembered, as if the house had finally started to decay. It was over one hundred years, he supposed. These places didn't live long once their occupant had passed away, as nature slowly crawled back after the footsteps had faded.

"Michael's here," he heard Molly announce.

"MICHAEL!" came a familiar voice, before people started to hush. That didn't stop his aunty though, as she bustled towards him from the other side of the kitchen, a tea towel in one hand and a great big grin on her face.

"Aunty Kathleen," he said, kissing her on her cheek.

"How wonderful to see you back,"

she grinned, before quickly adding, "Even under the circumstances." She eyed him up and down, peering out through tired, heavy-lidded eyes. She'd aged a great deal in the past few years. Her skin was loose, coated in a web of soft lines and wrinkles. Her once-auburn hair was now almost completely grey. She also seemed to have lost weight, like him, which only amplified her hunch. "How much you've changed! Have you been eating at all? Would you like a sandwich?"

"No thanks," he said. "I'm really not that–"

"WOULD SOMEBODY MAKE HIM A SANDWICH?" she shouted, ignoring him.

More hushes came from the corner, but his Aunty Kathleen didn't seem too bothered, or else she couldn't hear. Most likely the former, knowing his aunties.

"Do you want a cup of tea with it?"

"Er..."

"AND A CUP OF TEA!" she bellowed. "Your Aunty Mary is just gone to fetch the priest to say a few prayers. We've been on our feet since six o'clock this mornin' – the pair of us. I always forget how much work people leave behind when they're dead. It's enough to kill any of us!"

"You're too kind," Michael said.

"Ah, stop your coddin'!" she howled, grabbing his arm tight and shaking it profusely. "There'll be plenty for you to do too I'm sure. We'll all want to hear a tune or two on the piano later, of course."

"No Aunty, r-really I can't," he stuttered, suddenly feeling lightheaded. Perhaps he had taken too many pills on the flight.

"Here, eat this into ya'," she ordered, taking a plate of sandwiches and pushing them into his hands. "Sit down there and we'll get you something to drink with that. Is it tea you want? Or maybe something else?"

"It's all fancy Lattes now for him," he heard Molly remark. Sniggering broke out from behind him as he fell into a vacant chair. He dared not look up. Dared not meet their eyes as blood rushed to his face. His heart started hammering again and his head continued to swirl. Maybe he shouldn't be here. Maybe he should have never come back at all. It was all a big mistake...

Someone dropped a mug of tea on the table before him, making him jump.

"Milk and sugar over there," he heard a voice say. "Are you alright? You look like you have a fever."

He had no choice but to look up now. Everyone would be watching.

"I'm fine," he said, trying to smile. A red-faced woman was peering down at him, clenching what looked like an egg sandwich in her hand.

Classic wake nourishment.

"Aunty Kathleen is telling us you'll be playing a song later," the woman before him mumbled, stuffing the sandwich into her mouth. It was the mother of one of his old classmates, he realised, but he couldn't remember her name.

"I'm not that good," Michael said.

"Don't be daft," the woman barked, pieces of scrambled egg wetting his face. "Your aunties are always going on about how great you are at playing. It would make them very happy."

"Ah, play us a tune, Michael," he heard Molly say from the other side of the kitchen. He wiped the egg from his face and turned around. She was sitting the other side of the table with two old classmates, Alan and Sinéad. "You were always the best."

"And her favourite too," Sinéad added, reaching across the table to grab a sandwich. He now recognised the red-faced woman as Sinéad's mother, and they seemed equally ravenous.

"No, I mean I haven't played in years," he lied, feeling beads of sweat forming underneath his heavy fringe.

Was he *really* his teacher's favourite?

He pulled at his jumper collar – it was getting too hot.

"Really, I'm not that good anymore." The last thing he wanted was to be stuck playing the piano all evening, especially without seeing his parents first.

"What? At the piano?" His Aunty Kathleen had returned, running around Sinéad's mother with a fresh plate of sandwiches in her hand. He hadn't even touched the first plate yet. He didn't think his stomach could take it, especially after watching mother and daughter devour them. "Sure isn't he playin' the feckin' piano beyond at Oxford!"

"Oxford?" Molly repeated, Sinéad cooing beside her.

"Yes, but it's all theory," he lied again. It was, at most, twenty per cent theory. "No actual piano playing."

"Sounds boring," Sinéad muttered, rolling her eyes behind a mug of tea.

"Excuse me, excuse me," came a voice behind Aunty Kathleen. It was his Aunty Mary, shorter and stouter than his Aunty Kathleen, but no less lively. A tall, bald priest followed behind. "We're going in to say a few prayers now with the family," she told the room, peering up through round glasses with thick, black frames. "You're all welcome to join and – Michael, is that yourself that's in it?"

Everyone turned to look down at Michael.

"Yes, I suppose," he said.

"Have you had anything to eat?" she asked, eyeing him up and down as his Aunty Kathleen had done. "Looks like you haven't had a morsel."

"Yes, I have," he lied. The sandwiches

before him had disappeared rather rapidly. Wakes were energy-draining events, he supposed.

"Well, that's good," she said, as others started to get up to leave. "You'll stay for some prayers, won't you? Your Aunty Kathleen and I would love that."

"Well, I really should be off to…"

"OFF?" Aunty Kathleen shrieked. "Sure, hasn't he only just returned? Our prodigal son!"

"Well, there you go, she's spoken," Aunty Mary said, marching towards the hall, the priest following. "Come on now, the lot of ye'!"

Repressing a sigh, Michael got to his feet, his Aunty Kathleen grasping his arm with a smile. He noticed her hands were just as veiny as the old lady's in the front room. Were his aunties now as old as her? The thought made his legs weak as he walked.

"When are ya' going back?" a whisper sounded next to him. It was Molly, taking his other side.

"Oh, well, after New Year's," he said; the very next day after the will reading in fact.

"Nice," she whispered. "A few of us will be heading to Dermot's on New Year's Eve. Do you want to come? Or are you too good for us now?"

"No," he replied, surprised by the sting in her tone. What was she implying? "I mean, I'd love to go, but..."

"But what?" she interrogated, eyeing him suspiciously.

"Well, I was planning to be with my parents," he admitted.

"Oh?" she said, startled. "On New Year's night?"

"Well, yes," he said. Surely most people wanted to spend New Year's with their family?

"Each to their own, I suppose," she commented.

They were back in the hall now, edging their way to the front room. It seemed everyone in the house had been summoned to prayers. He'd never seen the house so packed before. More people had been outside apparently and were now trying to push the front door in on the already-crammed hallway. Warm breaths tickled his neck, making the hairs rise.

"Come here to me, what do you make of all that UK border nonsense?" Molly asked.

"Well, I try not to give it much thought, to be honest."

"Why not?" she inquired. "You're not for an even more divided Ireland, are ya'?"

"No, of course not!" he snapped. Why was she asking all of this? He took a breath and tried to remain calm, focusing on his aunty's hands clutching his arm.

"Alright," she said, smirking. "It's just, you never know about those people who leave this land to go over there. Honestly, I don't know what that country has to offer that they can't find here."

Michael paused for a moment, pondering what she'd just said. "What's that supposed to mean?" he then asked. "Those people? What people?"

"Well, you know what they say about them?"

"No, actually, I don't," he said, feeling his heart rate increase.

"Tell me you don't remember your Irish Lit?"

"Look, I don't know what you're talking about, Molly."

Then, taking his other arm and leaning in close to his right ear, so close he could feel her warm, sweet breath, she whispered, "West Brit!"

His head jerked, and he stared into her eyes. He could see she was trying to suppress a smile, but it only broke across her face into a grin. He was just about to reply when his aunty heaved him into the front room.

The priest was already standing at the foot of the coffin, a small prayer book open in his hands. He followed his aunty behind a row of chairs towards the corner of the room, where they stood. Michael watched as people slowly filed into the room, gathering around the coffin. Some stood outside the door. He couldn't make out where Molly had gone, not that he wanted to meet her eye; more so that he could avoid it.

The room was almost full, so full he could hardly see the outline of the coffin anymore, only the priest standing before it. The lady who had gripped his hand earlier was lighting a candle beside him. She placed the candle on a small table, where he also spotted a bowl of holy water. When she had taken her seat, the priest cleared his throat.

"We gather here, family and friends, and all those who have loved, to honour, respect and to pray..."

Michael watched his purple lips move, bulging with each movement, as if they were about to burst and spray blood all over the deceased.

"...and now that the soul has gone from us and into the Lord's presence, we also come into the Lord's presence to remember and give thanks..."

Spit sprang from his lips with each utterance, wetting his teacher's black, polished shoes.

"She could be watching us," came his mother's voice in his head. "Her soul could still be trapped inside."

He wondered then if she was still in there, listening to this priest speak and the quiet coughing from the other side of the room. He looked up to see a hand over Molly's mouth. She caught his eyes and frowned.

"I invite you all now to say one decade of the rosary," he heard the priest say. Everyone around him made the sign of the cross, which he then performed quickly, feeling Molly's gaze burn into his forehead. "I believe in God, the Father almighty, creator of heaven and earth," the priest began, Michael moving his lips but not quite issuing any coherent word. Instead, he wondered how long this would go on for. Perhaps he should have left the house once he had shaken everyone's hands as he'd originally planned, unless he'd found his parents. But no, he had had to say yes to Molly, and yes to his Aunty Kathleen and yes to his Aunty Mary. But all this was undoubtedly expected from him. And now he was walking right into the midst of it, and possibly ten Hail Mary's.

"On the third day he rose again. He ascended into heaven," the priest rattled on, his purple lips wet and shiny in the candlelight. There was no getting out of this now – he was in deep. What if she was trapped too, inside her body? Would she want to listen to all these prayers? Wasn't music her prayer?

"Why don't you join the choir,

Michael?" came her voice in his ear, just as loud and clear as it was in that lesson.

"I think I'd prefer to stick to the piano, actually," he'd responded.

"I bet you have a lovely voice in there," she'd smiled, pulling a cigarette from the packet and leaning over the piano to light it, the sun shining in the window behind her. "It would be a shame for God not to hear it."

"It's probably best if God didn't hear it," he'd replied, stuffing his pencil and manuscripts into his schoolbag as quick as he could – he'd always wanted to leave as soon as a lesson had finished. But suddenly, he'd felt her hand grasp his wrist.

"Are you sure?" she had asked in a deep, gravelly voice, her long fingers wrapping around his tiny wrist. "It would be a shame if I told your parents how naughty you've been. What you've been doing." He'd tried to release his arm, but her hand was too tight. Too strong. It was then he remembered how small and feeble he was. "Look at me, Mikey." He'd kept his eyes on his wrist, watched the white skin stretch tight over her bony knuckles, gleaming in the spring sunlight. "Look at me," she had repeated, as he felt his arm go numb.

"LOOK AT ME!"

He opened his eyes to see her skeletal face staring out at him from the coffin. Her white eyes bulged from her skull. He let out a scream, before throwing a hand over his mouth to silence it.

"Michael!" he heard his Aunty Kathleen hush. He turned around to see people frowning at him as they prayed. He pretended to cough into his hand, before clearing his throat.

Couldn't they all see her? Why was it only him?

He looked back to the coffin, only to find more people standing in front of him, blocking his view. He tried looking over their shoulders but, even then, he could barely see the coffin's outline.

How had he seen his teacher then, if he could barely see the coffin?

But he had heard her voice – he was sure of it. He had forgotten that voice for some years, and yet it sounded so loud, so clear. Had he kept her voice alive in his dreams perhaps? No, he decided. He never heard her in his dreams. Whenever he entered this house, he would wake up screaming and coated in sweat, the mattress damp around him. He was lucky he didn't have to share with a roommate – one perk of a music scholarship – who would no doubt be woken numerously in the night to his head-splitting screams.

"Our Father, who art in heaven," the priest continued. He desperately wanted to leave the room now, not because he would soon find himself in the middle of ten Hail Mary's, but because of the fear of catching sight of his teacher's face again. He wanted to be as far away from her corpse as possible. Perhaps just standing near it was bringing her face and voice vividly to mind. That was enough reason to leave.

He looked to his right, but couldn't see a clear path to the door. There was no possible way he could disguise himself leaving. He would have to endure many disgruntled faces. He looked around to see Molly's eyes on him. She knew what he was up to. Knew what he was planning. He looked closely at her lips, which appeared to repeat the same two syllables over and over again: "West Brit! West Brit! West Brit!"

He had enough. Enough of Molly's judging eyes. Enough of his teacher's corpse. He had had enough with the whole room and their relentless praying. He couldn't endure it anymore. He had to get out.

"Excuse me," he whispered.

His Aunty Kathleen looked up and frowned, before taking a step back to allow him to pass, her lips still mouthing every word of the prayer. More faces shot angry looks at him as he passed, their prayers growing louder and louder as he moved towards the door.

"Lead us not into temptation, but deliver us from evil," they prayed.

"Sorry," he said, nearing the door. "Need the loo."

"It's upstairs," an old farmer with a big red nose shouted over the prayers, the smell of whiskey exuding from every bulging pore.

"Thanks," Michael said, looking towards the stairs.

"On ya' go, son," the farmer said, before belting, "AMEN!"

He hurried from the front room, feeling the farmer's eyes on the back of his head. To his left was the front door, the snow whizzing outside the coloured glass. But to his right stood the stairs, tall and dark, as it had always looked.

Should he leave the wake now, or wait for his parents to join? Would they still be at home? Or were they delayed with the snow?

He glanced over his shoulder to see the red-faced farmer pointing furiously to the stairs with his thumb. He could neither leave the wake, nor return to it. Not now. He'd have to pretend to use the loo first.

Michael smiled and nodded, before turning towards the stairs.

He suddenly felt five years old again, when his mother kissed him on the forehead before leaving him to his first lesson. A girl had jumped the steps before him, a great mass of curly brown hair bopping on her head, her footsteps echoing around him. She'd stopped on the last step, brushing the hair from her face.

"Oh, hi Michael," she'd said.

"Hi Molly," he'd replied with a smile.

"Come on," a hoarse voice had called from the top of the stairs. He'd looked up to see a pair of black shoes peeking out from underneath a long, dark grey skirt.

"Miss Callahan is waiting," Molly said, biting her lower lip. "See you tomorrow."

"Bye," Michael waved awkwardly, as Molly skipped past him to the door.

"Hurry up now," the voice shouted. He clutched his notebook and pencil and grasped the bannister, before pulling his little leg up onto the first step. He could hear the teacher's shoe tapping the hard, wooden step, each tap louder than the last.

Tap, tap, tap.

"Coming, Miss Callahan," he called, as he climbed the remainder of the steps.

Tap, tap, tap.

Finally, he came to the top, but no one was there. A closet door creaked open before him.

"Miss Callahan?" he called, peering inside.

Was she in there? Hiding?

"Miss Callahan?" he asked again, approaching the open door. He had thought he could hear crying. A very quiet cry.

Was it another student, hiding? Waiting to be picked up?

"Hello?" he asked.

Who could be inside?

He could hear them sniffle, before their crying stopped.

"It's just me," he said, reaching for the handle to pull the door open fully to let some light in. "It's just Michael."

He felt the cold handle on his fingertips when the door slammed shut, releasing a gust of air that blew him backwards. He grasped for the bannister before his foot slipped on the polished surface.

Suddenly, he now found himself standing on the edge of the top step, looking down. He gripped the bannister tighter, afraid that he would fall down the many steps, his head beginning to spin. How on earth had he got up there?

He looked around to find the closet door still shut. The hallway before him was in complete darkness. He couldn't see anybody. He couldn't hear a thing.

Had he really heard someone crying inside just then? Or had he just imagined it? A memory, perhaps?

A cold draft swept his cheek.

A window must be open, he thought. Who'd leave a window open on the coldest night of December?

Finally, he let go of the bannister and stepped forward, passing the closet door. The first floorboard creaked. He didn't remember any floorboards creaking up here. Perhaps they too were decaying, just like everything else in the house. The draft brushed over his whole face now, parting the long fringe from his forehead. Who'd be stupid enough to open a window? he wondered, as he continued down the hallway.

A door was wide open opposite him. Her room. "I don't want you exploring any rooms," came her voice. "Especially that room there. It's strictly out of bounds. You may only use the bathroom and the music room. That's all. Do you understand?"

"Yes, Miss," he'd said, without looking up at her face.

"Miss what?"

"Yes, Miss Callahan."

She had opened the door next to him. A long window appeared inside, with two armchairs in each corner. On the ceiling, high above him, hung a crystal chandelier, bathing the room in a warm, golden light. And to the right, just inside, sat a big black piano, a long bench lodged underneath.

"This is where we'll play," Miss Callahan had said. "So long as you behave acceptably."

The coldness in her voice had made him shudder.

The room was shrouded in darkness now. He flipped the switch, but no lights came on. A curtain fluttered on the window opposite, where the draft emanated. The black piano was still there, now covered in a film of dust, the bench tucked in underneath.

He crossed the room, brushing away some cobwebs that swayed from the chandelier, and pulled back the curtains. They felt wet, damp. He supposed the heating hadn't been turned on much upstairs. The moonlight hit his eyes, making him wince. Snowflakes darted past. The whole country must be covered in snow now, he thought. He hoped it would stop soon, or else he wouldn't be able to fly back at all.

Did he want that? Did he want to

spend more time here, at home, with his parents? He'd wanted to go to Oxford as quick as he could, focus his mind on his music and books. But now that he was here, in the remotest region of Ireland, it would be tempting to stay, spend some more time with them. Maybe even spend some time with Molly.

Perhaps he shouldn't have fled this life. His home. Perhaps Molly was right. What could he have in England that his own country couldn't offer? He could have always gone to study at Trinity instead of Oxford. He had the option. The scholarship was there on the table. But he had felt an urge to leave. A strong need to pack his things and get as far away as possible. As quickly as possible. Leave everything behind. Forget all about the...

But all he could remember was the snow.

The window was still open. His body ached; the room was freezing. He pulled down the window, his fingertips sinking into the soft wood, before shutting it with a solid bang.

He wiped his wet hands on his trousers and turned around. Moonlight illuminated the many corners and edges of the room. A piano leg gleamed. Perhaps he would be able to see the piano keys in the moonlight. Would they hear him, downstairs? Regardless, he crossed to the piano and pulled out the bench. He gave it a wipe and blew the rest of the dust away, making him sneeze, before sitting down and lifting the heavy lid. The keys inside also needed a good wipe, although he didn't bother with that for now. Instead, he sat up straight and placed his fingertips on the keys, exactly how she would have wanted him to, and knew at once what he should play.

He watched as his fingers swiftly led into The Lass of Aughrim – her favourite. He hadn't played it in years. Often, she'd request this at the end of a lesson and would always sing along in her best Irish tonality: "If you'll be the lass of Aughrim, as I am taking you mean to be, tell me the first token, that passed between you and me."

As he played, he felt his right shoulder tighten. He shook it off, supposing it was the chill in the room, and continued to play.

"Oh Gregory, don't you remember, one night on the hill," came her voice, almost as if she was standing behind him. Leaning into him, like she always did. "Come tell me the last token," she cooed, squeezing both his shoulders now. He felt his muscles tense. His heart was racing, out of rhythm, out of sync.

His finger almost slipped.

"Come tell me the last token," she whispered, breathing softly on his neck. The hairs on his ear tingled as she whispered, "Mikey."

He jumped and hit his knee against the piano leg, causing the lid to close with a loud bang. The dust from the lid blew into his face, into his eyes, and he almost fell backwards off the bench.

"Michael?"

He wiped the dust from his eyes and looked around. It was Molly, a hand over her mouth, as if hiding a smile.

"Oh, it's you," Michael said.

"Yes, it is," she said. "Who else would it be? A ghost?"

"No one, sorry," he said, wiping the dust from his sleeves and trousers. "Sorry, it's just this place gives me the shivers."

"I'm not surprised," she said, looking at the cobwebs dangling from the chandelier. "What are you doing up here anyway? Are you alright?"

"Yes," he said instinctively. "I'm alright."

"I thought you said you couldn't play anymore?" she questioned.

"Well, I am quite rusty."

"Quite?" she repeated, curiously.

"That's why I thought I'd give it a try," he explained, turning around to face her with a smile. "Especially if my aunties want me to play later."

"They were only coddin' with ya'," she laughed, waving a hand. "Come on downstairs. They've all stopped praying now, thank God!" Then, raising a finger to her lips, she whispered, "We've also got some sneaky poitín in the kitchen."

He pondered the word for a moment. Listened to its beat in his head. *Poi-tín.* That was a word he hadn't heard for years. Alien to his classmates at Oxford, no doubt. Almost alien to himself.

"Did ya' hear me?"

"Yes," he answered, nodding. "Poitín."

"You're not away with the fairies, are ya'?" she asked, folding her arms inquisitively, her eyebrows raised.

"No," Michael replied, shaking his head furiously. Then, looking up, he asked, "What fairies?"

"Oh Jesus!" she howled. "Come on. Let's get some poitín into ya'." She turned on her heel, her hair bobbing off her shoulders. "What fairies?" he heard her repeat, as she headed back down the stairs. He listened until her footsteps faded, until the silence crept back into the room.

Minutes passed, until he became aware of a light tap from the window. He turned around on the seat. The snow looked heavier now, the flakes almost coating every inch of the glass, blocking any moonlight that had shone through. Slowly, his eyes adjusted to the dark, to the near pitch black, until he could see the outlines of an armchair forming in the corner. He gazed further into the corner, into the depths of the chair, and wondered.

The room grew quieter and quieter,

the tapping on the window gently fading, sinking into the background. All he could hear now was his breathing. Except now, his breathing sounded hoarse. He could also hear a deep rattle in his chest, like a smoker's chest.

He closed his eyes and listened to his breathing closely, but the more it slowed, the louder the rattling sounded. He held his hand to his chest, pressing down his palm. It didn't feel any different. He didn't feel any rattle.

How could this be?

He opened his eyes. The room was still empty. And yet the hoarse breathing continued. The sound grew louder, as if someone was gasping for breath. It was close, in the same room. There was gasping from the corner, like someone was being strangled. He looked even closer, but there was no one there. And yet the gasping continued, louder now, just before him, until someone gasped from the armchair. Their last breath:

"MIKEY!"

He jumped to his feet and stumbled backwards, reaching for the doorframe, but hitting the switch instead. The chandelier crackled and burst into light. He grabbed the doorframe for support and looked up. The room was empty. The breathing had stopped.

Nobody was there.

He wiped the sweat from his forehead. Maybe Molly was right. Maybe he was away with the fairies after all. He flicked the switch and left the room in darkness, before heading downstairs to rejoin the wake.

II

He heard laughter and chatter coming from the front room. The alcohol must have been flowing generously now.

It had just gone ten, he noticed, checking his watch. His parents must be inside now, he thought. Wondering where he'd gone.

"There you are," came Molly's voice before he felt her hand on his arm. He found himself being pulled down the hall and into the kitchen. "They're all in the back," she said, smiling over her shoulder, her emerald eyes twinkling. "But don't worry, there's plenty left."

"Thanks, but I really should head back in," he said. "I was just about to check-"

"Just one drop," Molly insisted, pulling him into the kitchen. They reached the back kitchen, where people were gathered around the sink, topping up their drinks with a clear liquid from a green plastic bottle. "Here, leave a drop for him," Molly shouted. "Greedy feckers."

Sinéad and Alan stepped out of the way, knocking their drinks back. Molly grabbed the bottle and poured it into an empty glass. "Brewed in the back of Paddy Finan's shed, just before the old fecker died," she said as she poured a generous amount, as if this detail would calm his nerves. The alcohol stung his eyes and tingled the hairs in his nostrils. "So it's quality stuff. What d'ya' want with it?" she asked, looking around. "Do we have any Fanta lads? Or would you prefer a coke?"

"I don't mind," Michael said, shrugging his shoulders. He'd never had poitín before. "Whatever you think will work best."

"Doubt it will make any difference," she said, grabbing a bottle of luminous orange Fanta before filling the glass to the brim, splashing the worktop. She handed it to Michael, spilling some of the mixture over the floor.

"Smells lethal," Michael commented.

"That's how ya' want it," Molly said,

running a dishcloth over the worktop. She was doing a bad job, Michael observed, as she missed most of the orange spots. Must already be tipsy. "Probably seventy percent alcohol, though you'd never know. Go on – get it into ya'!"

He held the bright orange liquid to his lips, the fizzy orange making his nose tingle, and sipped. It was strong, but didn't taste too bad. The Fanta was probably more lethal.

"How is it?" Molly asked, leaning forward.

"Not too bad."

"Wait til' it hits."

Before he could take another swig, he felt his stomach burn. "Christ!" he said, placing a hand on his hollowed stomach. "That's strong." The burning spread inside him, all the way up to his throat.

"I told ya' it was quality stuff," she said, grinning. "Although some say it causes blindness."

"Blindness?" he repeated.

"I'm only coddin' with ya'," she grinned.

He took another mouthful and felt his

insides burn as it passed through his stomach. "That's enough," he said, wiping his lips and placing the glass on the worktop.

"Pussy!" Molly laughed, before knocking back half her glass. "Here, have more Fanta," she said, reaching for the bottle.

"No," Michael said, waving his hands. "I really must head back inside. And I have to drive."

"You're not driving after that!" she said, her eyes widening as she topped up the glass.

"It's fine, it's not far," Michael insisted, feeling his head go light and his stomach lurch. He should have eaten those damned sandwiches. It'd been weeks since he last ate something substantial. "Maybe I'll walk."

"Good," she said, filling his glass with more Fanta. "Take that with you. You could be ages in there."

"Cheers!" he smiled, taking the glass.

"Don't cheers me!" she scowled as he turned to leave. "You West Brits!"

He left her in the back kitchen and placed his glass of orange poitín in the corner of a bookshelf, glancing over his shoulder to make sure she didn't see. Satisfied, he headed back to the front room, which he found to be surprisingly full, despite the late hour. He then remembered how these wakes went on all night, until five or six in the morning sometimes. He often wondered how it felt to have your house packed with people when all you wanted to do was grieve in solitude. Or was it necessary to have all your friends and family there, all your loved ones, to help pass what would otherwise be a long and sleepless night? Was there some mysterious, ancient logic to these late-night shenanigans? Was a wake, after all, the best way to mourn?

Or maybe it wasn't all about those who'd been left behind. Maybe the parties were to keep the dead entertained through an otherwise long and lonely night. He'd once heard his father say the dead could never be left alone in the house. "T'would be disrespectful," he'd said at one wake when Michael was a teenager. "T'would be bad luck. You wouldn't like to be left alone either, would ya', if you were dead?"

He couldn't think of anything lonelier.

"Michael," he heard his Aunty Kathleen call.

She was sitting in the opposite corner with his Aunty Mary and the priest, cradling a mug of tea. "Where have you been? You missed Father Brennan's lovely sermon. It was all about Irish hospitality, especially in times like this. Wasn't it lovely, Mary?"

"Aye, t'was lovely."

"Lovely!" his aunty repeated excitedly. "Take a seat there, won't you?"

"Thanks, but-"

"I hope you haven't stopped saying your prayers," his Aunty Kathleen interrupted, eyeing him as he scanned the room.

"No, it's not that," he explained. "I just needed the loo earlier. And then I got a little side-tracked."

"Suppose it's been a few years now since you were here last," his Aunty Mary said, looking away from the priest. "Must bring back a lot of memories for you?"

"It does," Michael said, preferring to forget. "Lots of memories. All good."

"I was just telling Father Brennan about the time you hid in the closet upstairs," Aunty Mary continued. "You must have been about six or seven. Just a gossoon."

The closet?

Michael felt for the chair as his legs swayed.

"His mother, my sister-in-law, came here to collect him, and I swear to God, didn't she find a surprise for herself."

"What surprise, Mary?" Aunty Kathleen asked, looking worried.

"Piss! Flooding down the stairs!" she yelled.

"WHAT?" shrieked Aunty Kathleen.

"Well, didn't his poor mother have to climb the whole stairs, only to find himself hiding in the closet upstairs crying, and pissing himself silly."

"Stop Mary!" Aunty Kathleen said, shaking her head. "The poor creature."

Michael sank back in the chair as legs failed him. He felt hot, sweaty. His breathing quickened. His head felt light. He tried to hold his breath and count.

One, two, three, four...

He steadied his hands on his knees, but he couldn't stop the shaking. There was nothing he could do to hide it. He could feel his trousers dampen beneath his hands. He could smell the alcohol oozing from his sweat.

...five, six, seven, eight.

"And that's not all," came a voice to his right.

He could sense everyone's head turn to look at the speaker. "Didn't I hear he used to touch all the girls? Oh yes. Fondle them, even!"

He could feel his whole body shuddering now. Even the floor was shaking under his chair, as if there was a tremor underneath the very floor.

Why had nobody else noticed it? Shouldn't they all be scared?

"My youngest daughter, Grainne, came home from school one day in tears, talking about a boy and his dirty little finger. I would have cracked it in two if I'd got my hands on him. Filthy little thing!"

"Filthy!" the red-faced farmer shouted from across the room, audibly drunk. The room cheered in response.

"Was that him?" he heard someone ask. All eyes would be on him now. There was no escaping. He leaned forward, tugging his arms around his legs. He hoped this would steady him in the chair as he tried to slow his breathing. But he couldn't slow it. They just wouldn't shut up. "Is that the boy who touched all the girls?"

"It is," the woman's voice confirmed. "Tis' himself."

It wasn't true.

"FILTHY!" the man shouted again.

"Disgusting!"

"And that's not the worst of it," the woman continued. He clenched his trousers tight. Felt his aunties' eyes all over him. "He even touched the boys too."

The room gasped.

"Is that why my Jimmy was crying?" another mother asked. "God, it must be over ten years ago. He said someone touched him!"

"Sounds about right," the woman said.

It wasn't me.

"The dirty boy."

"Dirty boy!" the room chanted.

"Shocking carry on," the woman to his right commented. "How many years has he been doing that? Ten? More?"

It's not true.

"Send him back!" the room sang.

"And where did he do all this?" some-one asked. "At school?"

"Aye," the woman confirmed. "Wher-ever he could get his dirty hands on them."

"My wee fella, Connor, he used to go to choir. After school on Tuesdays and Thursdays. He was never right after those evenings. Used to come home, his face pale and scared-looking. He wouldn't say a word for days. Do you think? You don't think-"

"It must be him," the woman said.

"You mean to say, he was doing it in our very church? Under our noses?"

"NO!" a voice cried. "Not my Johnny?"

"My Siobhan?"

"You dirty little-"

"IT WAS HER!" Michael screamed, jumping to his feet. Aunty Kathleen's mug slipped from her fingers, spilling tea all over the cream carpet, staining it a rich dark brown. "It was her! She touched all your children. It wasn't me! It was all her doing!"

"Who, my dear boy?" he heard his

Aunty Kathleen ask.

"He must be mad," someone said.

"It was her," Michael said, pointing towards the coffin. "It was Miss Callahan."

"Miss Callahan?" his aunty asked. "Your teacher?"

"Yes," he stated.

"But there's no Miss Callahan here," the woman behind him said. For a moment, he thought he hadn't heard her correctly.

"What?" he asked, not taking his eyes off his aunty.

"He must be pure mad."

"Aye, can happen to the best of them."

"Michael?" his aunty asked, looking up into his eyes, taking his trembling hands in hers. "Are you sure you're alright?"

"I am alright!" he shouted, seizing his hands from her, stumbling backwards. "It was her," he repeated, pointing towards the coffin where a couple of people were sitting, clutching their drinks. But instead of seeing his teacher lying dead there, someone else had taken her place.

"No," he said, stumbling towards it. Perhaps he wasn't seeing clearly.

"Some say it causes blindness," came Molly's voice. He looked over his shoulder, but she wasn't there. Or, he couldn't see her.

He gripped the edge of the wooden coffin for support, steadying himself, before peering down at the young, pale, fresh face. His long brown hair had been washed and parted, possibly even blow-dried, revealing a smooth, rounded forehead. His cheeks looked a little ruddier than usual, as if someone had applied blusher. And his lips were slightly pouted, almost smiling. There were no dark circles under his eyelids. Even the scars on his knuckles had faded, no longer a faint red. His smooth hands were resting on his chest, his stomach too sunken to support them. He looked like he was sleeping. Restful.

At peace.

He rubbed his eyes. He couldn't believe what he was seeing. His corpse was wearing one of his father's light beige suits, he could tell. He'd never owned a suit while in Ireland, not since his confirmation, having skipped his school graduation. He spotted his father's deep purple tie and pocket square, which he'd only seen him wear twice, to his communion and confirmation. Now they were back for his next rite of passage.

His own wake.

"No," he repeated, stepping away from the coffin. He turned around to face his aunties. "Where are my parents?" he asked. "Are they okay?"

"They're fine, Michael," his Aunty Kathleen said. "They'll be here soon, so there's no need to worry."

"I think you should sit," the priest next to him said. He turned to look at the old bald man, his eyes gazing at him from two dark sockets. "This must be a lot to take in."

"Get him a drink," his Aunty Kathleen called to the room.

"A cup of tea, maybe?" his Aunty Mary chimed.

"No," Michael said, stumbling backwards into the coffin.

"A cup of tea will do you good," his aunty said.

"I DON'T WANT A CUP OF TEA!" Michael roared, running his hands through his hair, scraping his face with his sharp, unkept nails. "WHAT THE FUCK IS WRONG WITH YOU?" he shouted at the room. Everyone stopped to look up at him. The farmer took a gulp of his whiskey. "WHY ARE YOU STILL DRINKING?" he screamed, looking around.

"It's your party," his Aunty Kathleen said with a smile.

He swung around, almost knocking the coffin.

"It's not," he said. "It can't be."

"This is why you've come home," she said. "Isn't it great?"

"But this isn't my house," he said. "This isn't my home."

"Well, it practically is," his Aunty Mary said. "You spent an awful lot of time here. Especially before... I mean, some even thought you were her son."

"No," he interrupted, shaking his head, moving towards the door. "You've all got this wrong. This isn't my wake. I'm not dead!"

He spun around, only to find the door blocked by mourners, all holding up a drink as he approached. Others were still eating sandwiches.

"We've been waiting, Michael," the suited man who had patted his shoulder earlier said, standing up from his chair. He still didn't recognise his face.

"MOVE!" Michael yelled, pushing his way through.

"He'll be back," he heard the man say as he fell out into the hallway. He stumbled, falling into the grandfather clock, before grabbing the bannister of the stairs for support.

What the hell was going on?

He could see the front door before him, snowflakes drifting past the coloured glass. He couldn't drive, at least Molly had said. But he could still walk home. Find his parents. Maybe they knew what was happening.

He pushed himself to his feet and, staggering slightly, bolted towards the front door. He grabbed onto the handle and pulled it down. It was jammed.

Frozen?

He continued to jerk the door handle, but it wouldn't budge. Had the snow frozen it completely? Could it do that? Still, he continued to pull it, pressing his feet into the bottom of the door.

Pulling.

Pulling.

"I wouldn't bother."

He glanced behind him to see Molly standing in the hallway, a bright orange drink in her hand. "You forgot this."

"I've had too much of that," he snapped, turning towards the door. "Here, help me open this. It's stuck."

"It'll be stuck for a while," he heard her say. She sounded closer now. He looked to see her standing by the door, staring out through the glass. "They say it's snowing all over Ireland now. There's no going outside."

"What the hell is going on Molly?" he asked, turning towards her. Her emerald eyes were wide and glassy. "Why are we stuck in here?"

"Didn't you hear me?" she asked, her brown eyebrows furrowed. "It's snowing."

"Fuck that," he said, banging on the door with his fist. His knuckles scorched with pain.

"Michael, you're bleeding," Molly said, taking his hands in hers. Blood streamed from his bruised knuckles, all the way down his arm.

"It's fine," he said, freeing his hands from her. "They bleed easily. Look, I'm going to try the back."

"Michael?" Molly called, running after him down the hall. "There's no use. We've already tried."

"Not hard enough!" he shouted back at her, as he stumbled into the kitchen. "MOVE!" he barked at those standing in front of the back door. They had the radio playing. Pop music, or something horrible.

"Freak," he heard someone say. Alan or Sinéad. It didn't matter. Nothing mattered now except getting the hell out of this goddamned house.

He reached for the handle and yanked it, only to find it just as frozen as the front door.

"You can't go out there," someone said behind him.

"I'm not spending the night trapped in here," he gasped, before falling backwards into the door. "Not with all of them."

"Molly, your friend's being weird," Sinéad said.

"Leave him alone," he heard Molly say. Just as he was about to sink to the floor, he grabbed the handle and got to his feet. "Michael?"

"I'm getting out of here," he said, pushing past them. "I don't care how, but I'm getting the fuck out of here. You can all stay with them."

"With who?" Molly asked, frowning.

"Those deniers!" he shouted at her. She looked stunned. Scared. "Come on Molly, it's hardly a secret."

"Shut up, Michael," he heard Sinéad say.

He looked over Molly's shoulder to find Sinéad hiding behind her glass.

"What about him?" Michael asked, looking towards Alan. He'd been quiet all evening, he'd noticed. His lips looked tightly sealed.

"We don't know what you're talking about," Molly said, biting her lip. Her eyes looked watery.

"You're just as bad the rest of them," Michael spat, before turning his back on her. He stormed through the kitchen, pushing chairs out of his way. If he couldn't get

out downstairs, the only other way was up.
But instead of the clear hallway he had expected, he found it crammed with people.

Not prayers again?

"Given up yet?" the man in the suit
asked.

"Fuck no," Michael snapped. "Move!"
He pushed the suited man out of his way,
only to feel hands grasping at his shoulders.
"Get off me," he shouted, pushing his way
to the foot of the stairs. But his shoe kicked
against the wooden step, and he was flung
headfirst into the stairs. He heard his forehead crack against the hard step, shooting
pain around his skull and down his spine.

"It would be a shame to see you go,"
he heard the man's voice say, only making
his head throb. "Your aunties went to great
lengths to put this all together."

He spun around to see Sinéad's
mother, the farmer, the priest and everyone
else standing at the foot of the stairs, staring
up at him. Beads of sweat ran down his face.
Tears streamed from his eyes. The mixture
wet the tip of his lips, leaving them wet.
Strong, like alcohol.

"Come on down," the suited man said,

holding out his hand. "At least stay the night."

"No," Michael said through gritted teeth, before getting to his feet and dragging himself up off the stairs. He wanted to leave now. He had to.

Finally, he reached the top of the stairs and looked down the hallway. Her bedroom door was still open. A bolt of pain erupted in his head, spreading through his body, causing him to scream. He could see stars before him, dancing up and down the hall. But someone was there. He could just about see them through the stars, inside her room. Sitting on her bed.

He squinted his eyes, pushing the stars away with his hand. It was a boy, around ten, perched on top of the bed. He was dressed in his school uniform: blue shirt, navy jumper and tie. The boy turned to look at him. Their eyes locked. His lips moved, mouthing the letter 'M'. But he couldn't hear him. The boy was talking, but he couldn't hear a word.

"What?" Michael asked, pushing himself forward.

The boy was screaming now, yelling

as loud as he could, and still all that Michael could hear was the deafening silence.

The boy's eyes widened. He looked scared. He seemed to be shrinking, as if the door and bedroom were growing high around him. Just as he was about to reach for the doorframe, a shadow appeared in the boy's eyes. The boy's mouth fell open in horror. His face turned white as snow.

Her.

"NO!" he screamed, grasping for the handle.

But the door slammed shut on the boy's screaming face. He pulled the handle, but it was stuck.

"No," he said, aware now that he was crying. He leaned back against the door, tears running down his face. He closed his eyes, felt the darkness enshroud him.

"It would be much easier if you came downstairs."

It was the man's voice again.

Who was he?

"I wouldn't stay up there if I was you."

"LEAVE ME ALONE!" Michael shouted.

Why wouldn't anyone just leave him

be?

He heard a door creaking before him. He looked up and saw the closet door at the other end of the hallway wide open. Again, he thought he could hear crying, only this time it was louder. Perhaps it was the child he'd heard crying in the front room? Perhaps he'd lost his mother?

He got to his feet and headed towards the closet, past the music room. The sobbing grew louder and louder with each step. He didn't dare look down the stairs, instead keeping his eyes firmly fixed on the back of the closet. Or at least what he thought would be the wall, since he couldn't see anything inside. Still, he could hear someone sobbing. It sounded like a child.

"Hello?" he whispered.

Almost at once the crying stopped. Whoever was inside had heard him.

"Who's in there?" he asked.

From the shadows emerged a pair of brown eyes, tears glimmering in the low light from downstairs. He looked up, his gaze fixed on Michael.

"What are you doing in there?" Michael asked, leaning forward.

The boy raised a finger to his lips. "Shh," he hushed.

"It's okay," Michael said, holding out his hand. "I can take you downstairs. Are your parents still here?"

The boy shook his head, keeping the finger to his lips.

"Well, I'm sure they'll come back," Michael said. "It's no use hiding in here. Come on downstairs."

But the boy shook his head furiously now, whispering something behind his finger.

"I can't hear," Michael said, leaning in closer.

Then, he caught a word.

"Coming," the boy said.

"Yes, I'm sure your parents are coming," Michael reassured him.

But the boy continued shaking his head, his mumbling growing louder.

"Coming, coming, coming," he repeated.

"Let's go downstairs, before they come," Michael said, reaching into the closet.

"NO!" the boy suddenly screamed,

looking into Michael's eyes. "SHE'S COM-ING!"

"Who?" Michael asked, taking a step back in case he was scaring the child.

"SHE'S COMING!" the boy repeated.

The words reverberated in his head as he took another step backwards, away from the screaming child.

"SHE'S COMING! SHE'S COMING!" the boy continued.

"Michael?" came a call from downstairs.

Michael turned to look, only to find his mother gazing up at him, her face white, and her brown eyes wide.

"Michael?" she called again, looking directly into his eyes.

"Mother?" Michael said, relieved. "There's a child up here, crying. I think he's lost his parents."

"Michael, I'm down here," she shouted, clutching her black handbag, staring up at him.

"I know," Michael shouted over the boy's muffled crying, confused. "But there's a child here. We need to find his parents."

His mother's eyes fell to the stairs, before she stumbled backwards into the wall, clasping a hand to her mouth. He looked down to see a stream of yellow liquid running around his shoes, running all the way down the steps to his mother. He turned around to find it coming from the closet behind him, only now the door was closed.

He looked down at his mother, who was picking up the bottom of her skirt.

"Michael, I'm coming," she cried, her shoes pounding on the hard, wet steps.

Michael stepped backwards to give her room, retreating down the hall, as he watched his mother reach the landing and throw open the closet door.

"MICHAEL!" she screeched, throwing both her arms inside.

"SHE'S COMING!" he heard the boy shouting at his mother. "SHE'S COMING! SHE'S COMING!"

He watched as two chubby hands were flung around his mother's shoulders, shaking as she pulled the child closer. Then, from behind her, he saw his own brown eyes, looking directly up at him.

"She's coming!" he sobbed into his mother's shoulder.

But she didn't do anything.

Nobody did.

"No," he said, stepping backwards, shaking his head. "It didn't happen to me. It never happened." It was just his imagination playing tricks with him, wasn't it? Dreams messing around with his mind. Wasn't it?

A cold draft swept the back of his neck.

The window.

Hadn't he already closed it?

"We're still waiting," came the man's voice downstairs. The unknown man was back again, and possibly with everyone else. "It's safer down here with us. I've even got more poitín."

"What?" Michael said, turning to look down the stairs.

The man smiled as he withdrew a hipflask from inside his jacket. "I only brew the best."

"Paddy?" Michael said, remembering the radio obituary. "But you're dead?"

"Aren't we all?" the man beamed, before taking a drink.

"Isn't this what you wanted?" his

Aunty Kathleen said, looking up at him. "Haven't you always wanted to be dead?"

Michael shook his head, before turning towards the empty hallway. It couldn't be possible. It was the poitín. It had to be the poitín – it'd gone straight to his head. Especially with the pills. That was it, surely? These people weren't dead, right?

Right?

He turned into the music room and found the window open again. He could climb through the window. It could be possible, as long as they stayed downstairs. He flicked the switch to his left, but no light came on. Not even a crackle.

Wasn't it working before?

Losing patience, he hurried across the room and threw back the curtains. The entire window was covered in thick snow, except for the small crack where the air seeped in. He pushed it up, the cold numbing his fingers. Except, it didn't move. The window, too, had frozen. He pushed and pushed, but the window stayed firmly intact.

"FUCK!" he yelled, before falling backwards. Every inch of the house was sealed.

Why was this so hard? How could snow do this to a house? "I should never have come back," he heard himself say, as he felt the seat on the backs of his knees. "I should never have left England."

Wasn't he a West Brit, after all, like Molly had said? He had wanted to say music was above politics, but that wasn't the whole truth. He had wanted to leave his country. But it wasn't because he was sick of it, nor did he prefer Britain. It was just the only way to escape.

He let his legs crumble and fell back onto the seat. His arm bumped along a few keys, playing a broken melody. He turned towards it, his head falling onto his chest, and closed his eyes.

He couldn't tell how long he sat there. All he knew was that with every second the room grew colder, his hands growing numb in his lap. He clenched them together, clasped them between his stick-thin thighs, hoping this would warm them.

A stale smell wafted beneath his nose. Cigarettes.

"Well, aren't you going to play me something?"

His body froze. His lips tightened. He knew that voice. How could he forget that voice?

A shiver ran down his spine, making his whole body shudder. Maybe he should have stayed downstairs. Maybe he was safer with them, no matter how insane they all were.

"You need to relax, Mikey," she said. "You were always a very nervous boy."

He opened his eyes to see her reflection on the surface of the piano. She was sitting behind him in the armchair, her head tilted to the side, watching.

"I'm waiting," she said, her voice clipped.

Her shoe tapped the floor.

He shut his eyes and dropped his head, wrapping his arms around his shuddering body. "This can't be happening," he whispered, hearing his lips crack. "It's just the drink."

Tap. Tap. Tap.

"This isn't happening."

Tap. Tap. Tap.

"It's just the drink. This isn't happening."

"What about my favourite?" she finally asked, the armchair creaking as she rose. "You remember the tune, don't you? The Lass of Aughrim? You liked that one, didn't you?"

"Go away," he said, shaking furiously on the seat. "You're not real."

"Just one song"

"Go away!"

"Please, Mikey."

"Go away! Go away! GO AWAY!"

He gasped for breath, the cold air piercing his lungs. He studied the reflection on the piano surface, but nobody was there. He let go of his breath and turned around. The armchairs were empty. The room was still. Only the curtains on the window fluttered. Nobody was there. Not even a sound from downstairs.

Had everyone left?

He spun around to get up, only to be whacked in the jaw with something hard. Miss Callahan stood tall beside the piano, her hand held out before his eyes, shaking, her other hand resting on the lid.

"Don't make me do this," she warned, her narrow pupils shimmering in the faint light from the window. He saw her lip curl, caught a glimpse of her brown teeth as she grinned.

"You were always a stupid boy too," she said, before slamming the lid shut. He jumped as he felt the lid crush his knuckles. His body convulsed in pain. But when he looked, he found his hands still resting in his lap. Bloodied, but unhurt. The scars on his white knuckles burned brightly, like they always did when he was afraid, angry or upset. "That would usually teach you to shut up."

He pushed himself away from the piano, the seat tumbling underneath him. "What are you doing here?" he asked, the pain fading from his fingers, but never quite fully.

"I'm always here," she said, leaning against the piano and lighting a cigarette. "This is my house, after all."

"But you're not dead," Michael said. She glanced towards him, the cigarette lighting her dark eyes briefly. "The people downstairs. They said this is for me. They said they've been waiting for me. And-," he stopped, his white face flashing in his head.

"It's me downstairs. Am I dead?"

"Well, this is a wake," his teacher said, blowing smoke into the air. "It would seem fitting." He watched the smoke waft through the cobwebs, towards the door.

"But you," he continued, pointing towards her. "What about you? Aren't you dead too?"

"Mikey," she said, her head tilting. "Who told you I would be dead?"

Michael paused, searching his memory. "I heard it," he started, struggling to remember now that everything was cloudy. "I heard it on the radio earlier," he explained, "and my parents mailed me a letter from your solicitor about a will."

She took another puff from her cigarette, clamped tight between her thin lips. "Your parents mailed you a letter?" she asked, blowing smoke into the air. Michael's nose tickled. "And you flew home, all the way to attend the wake of your dear old teacher?"

"No," Michael firmly stated, shaking his head. "I didn't want to come here. They asked me to."

"How sad!" she gasped, pressing her

hand to her chest. "You didn't have to say."

"I'm sorry," he said, before realising it. "Look, I'm not here just for this."

"Then why are you *really* here, Michael?" she asked, her eyes examining him. "You can tell me. You can trust me."

"I always come home around Christmas now," he explained. "But this, this was all just coincidence."

"Then who else were you here to see?" she asked, squashing her cigarette into an ashtray on the piano.

But Michael couldn't concentrate, his eyes fixed on the cigarette. Where had the ashtray come from? And how was all of this happening?

"I, I come home to see my parents," he said, looking up at her. "I always come home to see my parents. As I said, around Christmastime."

"And where are your parents now?" she asked, her black eyes probing him.

"I don't know," he admitted, before remembering. "I think my mother's downstairs. I think I just saw her."

"Mikey," she said, stepping away from the piano.

"Stay back!" he warned.

"I hate to be the one to break it to you but, they're not here," she said, smiling. "It's just you and me."

"Stay away!" he shouted, taking a step towards the door. He'd be safer downstairs. He had to trust them, especially if his mother was down there now.

She turned to face him, moonlight illuminating the edges of her black hair, tied up into a tight bun. The window darkened behind her as more snow settled.

"Don't come any closer," he said.

She paused, resting her hands on her skirt.

"You're not going to leave me again, are you?" she asked. "You're not going to leave me all alone?"

"Fuck you," he spat, feeling for the doorframe.

"I'll tell everyone you've been an awfully naughty boy," she said, taking a step towards him. The hard tap echoed around the room. She looked taller again, looming before him, as she did many years ago. "Because that is what will happen, Mikey, if you don't stay a little longer. I'll tell everyone. I'll start rumours. I'll tell lies. The children will spread them. I've done it before – I can do it again. Now, give me your hand."

"LEAVE ME ALONE!" he shouted.

"I'll even show you my secret room."

"No," he said, covering his eyes with his hands.

"Come on, Mikey?" he heard her hiss, her breath on his lips: stale cigarettes. It grew more and more rancid with each husky breath. Rotten. Like all the rancid corpses he had smelt as a child at wakes, now contained in her breath. "After all these years, we're here, student and teacher, reunited. At last."

He felt her hands clasp onto his belt. Heard his fly unzip. "Good boy," she whispered, as she reached inside with her cold, clammy hands. "Stay still, and I won't tell your parents."

He felt his heart drumming against his chest, desperate to escape his little body. He too wanted to leave his body, be as far away from her as possible. His breathing came loud but quick, growing shallower with each breath of cold air. His chest started to pain him now. He knew there was no getting away. He never could. There was only one way to stop it.

He closed his eyes and slowly inhaled.

One, two, three, four...

Still, his chest continued to stab. He had to keep counting.

...five, six, seven, eight.

It wasn't working. He tried to move, to go back downstairs where it would be warmer, but found he couldn't: his feet were firmly stuck to the floor. He had frozen, like every other thing in the house.

"There's no leaving me now, Mikey," his teacher whispered in his ear, as her cold, damp fingers brushed his inner thigh. His heart froze. His breathing stopped. And still, she whispered: "It'll just be you and me up here. You and me, forever."

"NO!" he screamed, falling backwards, his back hitting something hard.

"Michael?"

"SHE'S COMING!" he shouted, his breath heavy. "SHE'S COMING! SHE'S COMING!"

Then he heard the sound of a door creaking. A breeze swept his face.

"Michael, what are you doing in

there?" he heard a familiar voice ask.

He opened his eyes to find Molly and everyone else looking down at him. He looked around, only to find stacks of towels on either side of him. He knew where he was. He'd hid in here many times before. Away from her.

"We thought you'd left," Molly said. She was standing in the hallway outside, an empty glass in her hand. "But then I found this lying on the stairs, empty, and I thought I'd come look for you. I heard you crying and shouting something, complete gibberish. It looks like you've had a bit much to drink. You had us all worried."

He looked around at all the people as he emerged from the closet. All their faces were white as snow, looking down at him in horror.

"Michael, what's happened your hands?" Molly gasped, pointing. He looked down to find blood trickling from his knuckles, the bitemarks jeering up at him. "You're covered in blood!" he heard Molly say. "Michael, are you alright?"

He wiped his fingers off his trousers before staggering to his feet. Molly moved to the side, as others shuffled down the stairs.

"Michael, I think you should come downstairs," Molly said, her voice quivering. "Please."

He spotted the suited man standing behind her. "Him," Michael pointed, taking a step towards the music room. "He's a ghost, Molly. That's Paddy Finan's ghost!"

"What?" Molly asked, swinging around. "Paddy Finan's brother?"

His Aunty Kathleen and Aunty Mary took a step forward, clutching rosary beads in their hands. They too were pale as ghosts, shadows of their former selves. They were all ghosts now.

A few light taps upon the window made him turn.

Tap, tap, tap.

The window was calling him, like it had done all evening, and he knew what to do. He darted across the room, headfirst into it. The curtains flew back as his head hit the glass, just below the timber rail. He felt the shards slash his face, slash his ears, as his whole body fell forwards, falling through the fluttering snow and glass, through the frozen surface of the road below. Falling sleepily through the snow, through the earth and the universe. Falling sleepily, sleepily...

*

He'd seen the car the moment they left the house, the tiny headlights almost masked by the heavy snowfall. But his parents hadn't noticed.

They never would.

"For God's sake, Peter, we have to tell someone," he heard his mother shout from the passenger seat. "His hands are bleeding, for Christ's sake!"

He cradled his battered hands in his lap, the blood staining his trousers, and watched the tears fall onto the open cuts. He winced as his knuckles stung, trying to forget the moment his teacher had slammed the lid on his hands before his mother found him crying at the bottom of the stairs. He'd never seen his teacher so angry before. But he'd deserved it. That's why he had tore into his knuckles with his teeth while waiting for this mother. He was the one who'd upset his teacher. He was the one who'd applied for the scholarships. Her pain was his to bear.

"It's only going to be a few more months," he heard his father say. "And then he's off to Trinity, or Oxford, or wherever he decides to go."

"It's not enough," his mother sighed. He opened his eyes. The car was closer now. Where were they going? Where were they rushing to in this weather? "She knows we know. She'll be expecting us to tell someone soon. We can't let this slip. Not this time."

"And who would we tell?" his father snapped. "The priest? Sure, he's just as bad as she is."

"What about his head teacher?" his mother asked. "Miss Callahan does a few classes there."

"But he'll be out of that school in a few months!" his father said.

"Would you slow down, Peter?" his mother shouted, grabbing the edge of her seat. "These roads are treacherous."

Michael stared into the mirror, the yellow headlights growing bigger, growing brighter. Perhaps he should tell them.

It almost looked as if they were gathering speed, and it made him uneasy. Dread built in the pit of his stomach. He knew something bad was going to happen. He'd have to tell them.

"Mam?" he whispered.

"Not now, Michael!" his mother snapped. "I'm trying to get your father to slow – what's that?"

"Looks like a tractor," his father said, leaning forward in his seat and squinting, the wipers desperately trying to remove the hardening snow from the window. "I can't see."

"Slow down, Peter!" his mother shouted, her nails digging into the seat cover.

"I CAN'T! THERE'S-"

The car suddenly appeared behind them. The headlights flashed in the rear-view mirror, blinding his eyes.

"PETER, SLOW DOWN!"

"I CAN'T SEE!"

The last thing he heard was the tractor beeping, before the car spun and crashed through a fence. They ploughed through the air and snow, falling forwards as the snow gathered on the windscreen, barricading the windows, barricading his ears, barricading his mind, until it was too late.

III

The front room was filling up quickly. He recognised some faces: Paddy Finan's brother, again dressed in a suit and, of course, his Aunty Kathleen and Aunty Mary, sitting next to each other in the corner. They looked distraught, their eyes red and dry from too much crying, rosary beads tightly entwined around their trembling fingers.

Someone approached him. He looked up to see Molly dressed in a smart black suit, her curly hair tied up and her emerald eyes brimming with tears. He watched as one tear escaped and ran down her cheek before wetting his skin.

Warm.

"Molly," he said, but she didn't reply. "Molly, please, listen to me!" he pleaded, but she didn't seem to hear him, like the rest of them. He wanted to tell her how everything was okay, how he was still here, that there was no need to cry. But no matter how hard he tried, they wouldn't reply. No one would reply.

He watched Molly bless herself, before she leaned over the coffin and kissed him on the forehead. Her lips were also warm. So different to the cold that had numbed his entire body, ever since he fell on the snow.

"Goodnight, Michael," Molly whispered in his ear.

"Molly," he called again. "Molly, please don't go. Don't leave me. You can stay. Don't-"

But she only wiped her tears with a tissue and left him for the door.

"Please," he cried. "Don't leave me. Please."

He didn't want to see any more people. He only wanted to see Molly. Have a laugh over the poitín about how drunk he'd got before falling. That's what had happened. He must've fallen on the snow and was now recovering. That's why they had come to see him.

"Poor lad," someone sniffed near his aunties, as others nodded sadly. "And didn't he look distraught all evening at Teresa Callahan's wake?"

"Couldn't get a word out of him," a red-faced woman said. Sinéad's mother. "And he wouldn't touch a sandwich either. He looked skeletal. Deathly. He mustn't have been right. They said he'd drunk the kitchen dry."

"He wasn't right in the head at all," someone said, "whatever was wrong with him. No one drinks that much poitín. I once had a drop myself and sure wasn't I away with the fairies. I thought I flew out of my own body."

"I don't think it was just the poitín, Mary," Sinéad's mother laughed.

He could hear others giggling.

"Ah well, we all have our demons."

"Aye, it's true, I suppose," Sinéad's mother said. "But he was a nice lad, really. Polite, like. Good on the piano too, they say."

"Aye, he'll be with his parents in heaven now, God bless him," an old farmer said.

"What happened to them?" someone Michael didn't recognise asked.

"Car accident, in the snow," the

farmer said, pulling a hipflask from inside his jacket before taking a swig. "Didn't see the car coming up behind them. Sped right into a ditch, bless them. Must be a few winters ago now."

"Oh Christ, is that their son?" someone gasped.

"Aye, tis' himself," the farmer confirmed, before taking a large mouthful.

"And what's going to happen the house?" someone asked, before whispering, "I heard she left it to him in her will."

"Did she now?" Sinéad's mother said, getting to her feet. "My daughter always said he was her favourite."

"Poor lad," the farmer said, blessing himself. "May they rest in peace."

It couldn't be true, Michael thought. He could hardly be...

People were leaving now. He could no longer see his aunties. In fact, he didn't recognise any of the figures heading towards the door. Where were they all going? Wouldn't they come back? He'd rather have these strangers around him than be left alone.

The front room had emptied. A floorboard creaked from upstairs. Soon, the whole house grew quiet. All he could see was the dim flickering from the candles at his feet.

Surely somebody would come to stay with him. Hadn't his father always told him the dead could never be left alone? Wasn't it disrespectful? Wasn't it bad luck?

A shadow fell upon the coffin. The candles sputtered before darkness swallowed the room. Someone new had approached. A waft of cigarette smoke passed his nose. It smelt familiar. Old.

Stale.

This can't be happening, Michael thought. It can't be her.

But he felt her cold breath on his ear.

"NO!" he screamed, hoping someone would hear him.

No one did.

She leaned in closer before whispering, "Hello Mikey."

ACKNOWLEDGEMENTS

I had this idea in my head for several years and made many failed attempts to turn it into a story. It wasn't until 2020 came along, and its months of quarantine, that I decided to revisit *The Wake*. But although 2020 gave me the time to delve fully into this story, it was ultimately the support of family, friends and colleagues that helped me see it through to the end. I want to thank my initial readers for reading the first hastily written, incomplete draft and responding positively: Liam Forbes (who corrected my spelling of poitín!), Emma Buckingham (and her eagle, editorial eye), Steff Young and all those who took to Zoom to tear it apart in a constructive fashion: Matthew Damsell, Adrian Smith, Veronica Allen, Victorine Pontillon and, of course, the host and partner in crime, Sean Sweeney. Without your honest feedback and criticism, I would still be struggling to find my way around this wake. Finally, I want to thank my family, and my community back home, for introducing me to the long tradition of the wake and teaching me the importance of celebrating life. The Irish certainly know a thing or two about how death should be approached and can help make this sometimes terribly difficult truth meaningful and, at the very least, bearable. Of course, Ireland is still a country struggling to come to terms with its past horrors, and my heart goes out to all those who have been through anything like what Michael has. To quote psychiatrist and author Bessel van der Kolk, "In order to understand trauma, we have to overcome our natural reluctance to confront that reality and cultivate the courage to listen to the testimonies of survivors."

ABOUT THE AUTHOR

NP Cunniffe was born in the West of Ireland and has an MA in Writing the Modern World from the University of East Anglia (UEA), Norwich. He is an Editor for a small publisher in London and has also published a children's picture book, *Scott and the Runaway Sock*, as Niall Cunniffe.

You can connect with me on:

https://www.instagram.com/npcunniffe/
https://www.facebook.com/npcunniffebooks/
https://twitter.com/np_cunniffe

Subscribe to my newsletter:

https://bit.ly/NPmailinglist

Made in the USA
Middletown, DE
05 March 2023

26251225R00064